The
Cats Gallery
of Art

The Cats Gallery of Art

SUSAN HERBERT

A BULFINCH PRESS BOOK
Little, Brown and Company
Boston · Toronto · London

Frontispiece

SIR JOHN EVERETT MILLAIS

1829-1896

Bubbles

First United States Edition
First published in the U.K. by Thames and Hudson Ltd., London

Library of Congress Cataloging-in-Publication Data

Herbert, Susan.
The cats gallery of art/Susan Herbert.
p. cm.
ISBN 0-8212-1798-4
1. Painting—Caricatures and cartoons. 2. Cats—Caricatures and cartoons. 3. English wit and humor, Pictorial. I. Title.
NC1479.H55A4 1990 89-29317
759.2—dc20 CIP

Bulfinch Press is an imprint and trademark of Little, Brown and Company (Inc.)
Published simultaneously in Canada by Little, Brown & Company (Canada) Limited

PRINTED IN SINGAPORE

FOREWORD

Professor Marmalade Katzenbogen

I have no way of knowing whether Susan Herbert is aware of the paper I published in 1949 (in the learned *Rundschau der Kunstgeschichte*) on the subject of the substitution of cats for the models in well-known paintings, but the pages which follow indicate at least an extraordinary sympathy of outlook. For Miss Herbert has unwittingly, or perhaps even wittingly, who knows?, demonstrated in a definitive way that my thesis, presented over forty years ago to the Faculty of Göttingen University, was not merely an example of academic fireworks – a form of twisting the lion's tail, as they aptly express it in Anglo-American circles – but a true and accurate hypothesis based on sound art-historical principles.

What I suggested in my by now famous treatise was that many of our Western masterpieces and favoured paintings might be viewed afresh if only they were repainted with cats instead of people. I held it for probable that if, for instance, the *Mona Lisa* were a furry feline rather than a smug human female, we would come much closer to Leonardo's primal impulses in undertaking that picture. And here, on page 11, is the proof!

In an elaborate painting such as Botticelli's *Birth of Venus,* with its wealth of Platonic undertones and hints of Renaissance allegory, surely the sheer beauty of the Goddess of Love as she emerges from the foam of the sea is a distraction from the philosophical scheme of the great work and its subtle allusions to Greek mythology. One look at page 8 will show how useful it is to overcome that distraction.

One does not have to be a rabid ailourophile to appreciate this gallery of paintings devoted to the independent, aloof, four-legged creatures who tolerate the company of human beings with barely concealed contempt. And yet, how charming they can be – as milkmaids, as aristocratic ladies, as kings and queens and cavaliers. . . Personally, I have always been partial to whiskers and fluffy tails, and a cat's purring is for me as sweet a form of music as Schubert's *Lieder*.

But I wander from the point. . . I recommend to you the pioneering work of Susan Herbert in presenting a gallery of famous and much-beloved paintings with a piquant difference. She has, as it happens, done me a professional service; but she merits a miaow of thanks from the general public too.

JAN VAN EYCK

c. 1390-1441

The Arnolfini Marriage

SANDRO BOTTICELLI

c. 1444-1510

The Birth of Venus

LEONARDO DA VINCI

1452-1519

Mona Lisa

HANS HOLBEIN THE YOUNGER

1497-1543

Portrait of Henry VIII

MARCUS GHEERAERTS THE YOUNGER

1561/62-1635

Portrait of Queen Elizabeth I

FRANS HALS

c. 1580-1666

The Laughing Cavalier

DIEGO DE SILVA Y VELAZQUEZ

1599-1660

Las Meninas

REMBRANDT HARMENSZ VAN RIJN

1606-1669

The Night Watch

JAN VERMEER OF DELFT

1632-1675

The Milkmaid

FRANÇOIS BOUCHER

1703-1770

Madame de Pompadour

SIR JOSHUA REYNOLDS

1723-1792

Lady Elizabeth Delmé and her Children

THOMAS GAINSBOROUGH

1727-1788

Blue Boy

THOMAS GAINSBOROUGH

1727-1788

Portrait of Mary Graham

FRANCISCO JOSÉ DE GOYA Y LUCIENTES

1746-1828

The Clothed Maja

JEAN-AUGUSTE-DOMINIQUE INGRES

1780-1867

Madame Moitessier

FORD MADOX BROWN

1821-1893

The Last of England

SIR JOHN EVERETT MILLAIS

1829-1896

Ophelia

SIR JOHN EVERETT MILLAIS

1829-1896

My First Sermon

My Second Sermon

HENRY WALLIS

1830-1916

The Death of Chatterton

ÉDOUARD MANET

1832-1883

The Balcony

ÉDOUARD MANET

1832-1883

The Bar of the Folies-Bergère

ARTHUR HUGHES

1832-1915

April Love

EDGAR DEGAS

1834-1917

Dancing Class

JAMES TISSOT

1836-1903

Colonel Barnaby

JAMES TISSOT

1836-1903

The Fan

CLAUDE MONET

1840-1926

Women in the Garden

AUGUSTE RENOIR

1841-1919

The Loge

JOHN WILLIAM WATERHOUSE

1849-1917

The Lady of Shalott

VINCENT VAN GOGH

1853-1890

Self-Portrait

---

overleaf

FRANÇOIS FLAMENG

1856-1923

Portrait of Princess Z. N. Yusupova